SKY WARRIORS

SKY WARRIORS

Aviation in the California Army and Air National Guards

René J Francillon

Published in 1988 by Osprey Publishing Limited
27A Floral Street, London WC2E 9DP
Member company of the George Philip Group

British Library Cataloguing in Publication Data

Francillon, René J
    Sky warriors: aviation in the California Army and Air
    National Guards.—(Osprey colour series).
    1. Aeronautics, Military—United States
    I. Title
    358.4′00973   UG 633

ISBN 0-85045-814-5

Editor Dennis Baldry
Additional photography Clay Jansson, William T Larkins,
Peter B Lewis and Carl E Porter
Designed by David Tarbutt
Printed in Hong Kong

Front cover Loaded with blue Mk 76 practice
bombs, two grey F-4Es and a green F-4C of the
196th TFS/163rd TFG, streak over the desert on
their way to the bombing range located 5 miles
NNW of NAF El Centro

Title pages An immaculate F-4D of the 194th
FIS/144th FIW, rolls out at the end of a training
mission at Fresno on 9 April 1987

Back cover On 21 May 1955, Lt John M Conroy
set a round-trip, coast-to-coast, record (5085
miles in 11 hr 26 min 33 sec, including six
refuelling stops) in this F-86A of the 115th
Fighter-Bomber Squadron. (*Clay Jansson via
Cloud 9 Photography*)

To the memory of the men and women of the California National Guard who gave their lives in the service of their state and country and in particular to Captain Dean Paul Martin and Captain Ramon Ortiz, of the 196th TFS/163rd TFG, and Major John Q Jordan, Jr, and Captain Wesley R Deane, of the 194th FIS/144th FIW, who were killed in flying accidents while this book was in preparation.

Units of the National Guard, the oldest military forces in the United States, are unique as they have status both as federal and state forces. Thus, in the case of California Air National Guard and Army National Guard units illustrated in this Osprey Colour Series book, Governor George Deukmejian is their current peacetime commander-in-chief whereas President Ronald Reagan would be their commander-in-chief if they were to be called to federal active duty.

The units trace their origin to the aeronautic unit which was formed on 12 March 1911 in the 7th Company, Coast Artillery Corps of the California Guard and the Aeronautical Section of the California Naval Militia which was mustered on 11 December 1915. However, neither received federal recognition and the true forebear of aviation units of the California Guard is the 115th Observation Squadron which was activated on 16 June 1924 at Clover Field, Santa Monica. Called to active duty on 3 March 1941, the 115th served during the war in the China-Burma-India theatre of operations. Re-organized in the California Guard as a bombardment squadron in October 1946, it is now the 115th Tactical Airlift Squadron and flies C-130E Hercules from the Van Nuys ANGB in the suburbs of Los Angeles.

Post-war, three fighter squadrons were also organized in California and a fifth ANG unit was activated in 1955. Separation between Air National Guard and Army National Guard resulted from the National Security Act of 1947 which created a separate Department of the Air Force, the overseer of ANG units. ArNG units were then placed under the much older Department of the Army.

I sincerely thank the California Military Department and the National Guard Bureau for their assistance and support and wish to express my sincere gratitude to my many friends in the California Air National Guard and Army National Guard for their warm hospitality.

René J Francillon
Vallejo, California, July 1987

Right Although this Beech U-8F Seminole used as a staff transport by the California Army National Guard is already 25 years old, it is immaculately clean and in perfect mechanical condition as the result of the care with which it is maintained by experienced AVCRAD personnel

Contents

Army Guard

126th Medical Company (Air Ambulance), 175th Medical Brigade. Sacramento Army Aviation Support Facility, Mather AFB.

California the beautiful. An UH-1V flies over the wooded shore of a reservoir in the Eldorado National Forest, between Sacramento and Lake Tahoe, during a training flight on 17 May 1987

Left Returning from a flight over the High Sierras, 74-22468 indulges in some NOE (Nap of the Earth) flying near the Rubicon River in El Dorado County. On this occasion the pilot was Captain Michelle North; when not flying a Huey for the Guard, she flies a JetRanger for a San Francisco radio station. Helicopter flying is a family affair as Michelle's husband is also an officer and pilot in the California Army National Guard

California oaks and an irrigated alfalfa field contrasting brightly with the dried natural grasses provide a colourful background for a Huey of the 126th Medical Company flying near Rancho Murietta in Sacramento County

The UH-1V designation identifies UH-1Hs which have been recently fitted with radar altimeter and DME (Distance Measuring Equipment). Most of the 25 Hueys assigned to the 126th Medical Company in early 1987 were of this variant

Overleaf Although this book was in no way sponsored by the Tourism Office, this view of an UH-1V flying over a recreational facility near the Rancho Seco nuclear generation plant appears to have been taken more to promote California's recreational facilities than to herald the might of the state's militia

All Army helicopters are now progressively repainted with a very coarse finish called CARC or Chemical Agent Resistant Coating. Although referred to as 'aircraft green,' the CARC shade used is almost black and reportedly has good radar and IR absorbent characteristics. As its name indicates, CARC is treated to make the removal of chemical contaminants easier and safer

Most first time visitors arriving in the winter or early spring safely assume that California was nicknamed the 'Golden State' after gold was discovered in the American River, some 45 miles east of Sutter's Fort—now named Sacramento and the site of the State Capital—on 24 January 1848. The nickname, however, comes from the fact that the native grasses turn yellow soon after the end of winter's rains, as shown in this photograph taken on 17 May 1987, and that most of the state's landscape is golden for eight months of the year. A hot air balloon drifting from a nearby field lends a touch of colour to this otherwise drab military scene

In performing its state mission, the 126th Medical Company (Air Ambulance) operates over a wide variety of terrain as California has both the lowest and highest points in the 48 contiguous states: Badwater, in Death Valley National Monument, is 280 ft/85 m below sea level, and Mount Whitney is 14,495 ft/4418 m above sea level. This photograph was taken in between these extremes on a cold winter day as Sgt Mi!o Luguna was winching a rescue litter down to a snow covered clearing at the 5500-ft level in the Eldorado National Forest, some 50 miles ENE from Sacramento

Native to Australia, the fast growing eucalyptus trees were first planted in California during the last century to serve as wind barriers. Drought-resistant, these trees soon spread through most of the southern half of the state. This nice specimen forms a fitting background for an UH-1V of the 125th Medical Company on detachment to Camp Roberts, the large California training base north of Paso Robles

49th Combat Aviation Company, Medium Lift Battalion, State Area Command. Stockton Army Aviation Support Facility, Stockton Metropolitan Airport

Flying low over typical high desert vegetation, this CH-47B (66-19124) was photographed in the Mojave Desert, a few miles north of the Air Force Flight Test Center at Edwards AFB, during a ferry flight from Camp Irwin and Camp Roberts

Overleaf Sun glinting from its canopy, this CH-47B hovers over a dirt road in the Mojave Desert. Had this photograph been taken during the summer or fall instead of on 14 March 1987 shortly after a rare desert winter rain, the Chinook would have been totaly engulfed in the dirt storm kicked up by its twin three-bladed rotors

17

Above Designed by the Vertol Aircraft Corporation in anticipation of an Army request for medium-lift helicopters capable of carrying a complete infantry platoon into combat, the Model 107 prototype of the Chinook was first flown in April 1958. The type, which is fitted with a rear cargo ramp for loading and unloading small vehicles such as jeeps, entered Army service four years later

Overleaf Crewed by 2Lt Diane L Belmessieri, CW3 George H Larson and SSgt Manuel J Cortez, 67-18452 tucks in close to the photo ship while bringing a platoon of California Guardsmen back to Auburn in the afternoon of 15 March 1987. First serving with the 129th ARRG of the California National Guard, Diane learned to fly helicopters at Fort Rucker, Alabama, after transferring to the Army National Guard. George flew Army helicopters in Vietnam and Manny had already served as a helicopter crew chief during the Southeast Asia War

A CH-47A being preflighted at Bicycle Lake,
Camp Irwin, by its 49th CAC crew

The peaceful arrival of the 'enemy': Guardsmen
disembark from a CH-47A of the 49th CAC to
take up position on the edges of the Keystone
Range. At dusk, they put on an impressive
firefight while 'attacking' the field facilities from
which UH-1Ms—one of which can be seen
facing the Chinook—of the 40th Attack
Helicopter Battalion were operating during a
drill weekend

Left In the spring of 1987, the 49th CAC was equipped with sixteen CH-47As and CH-47Bs but was receiving the first of the CH-47Cs with which it is to be fully re-equipped within the next two years. As more CH-47Cs are received, crews from the 49th are ferrying the older helicopters back to the Boeing Helicopter Company plant in Pensylvania, where they are rebuilt to CH-47D standards for assignment to active Army units and, later, to Guard units

Providing pilots with good visibility forward and downward, the lower glass panels in the CH-47 nose give the Chinook its distinctive grin. The barren hill in the background overlooks the helicopter field on the sands of Bicycle Lake, the largest of several dry lakes at Camp Irwin in the Mojave Desert

The nickname of the 49th Combat Aviation Company, *Delta Schooners*, appropriately blends references to the location of its home base—Stockton, one of California's two inland seaports in the Sacramento-San Joaquin Delta—and to the fact that the rotor masts of its Chinooks are configured like the masts of old sailing schooners—the aftmast being taller than the foremast. The fact that Schooner, the unit's call sign, is also the name of a large beer glass is believed to be purely coincidental. Nevertheless, for the crew of this CH-47A, seen returning to its home base at the end of a drill weekend, it soon will be time to enjoy a schooner or two . . .

27

**40th Attack Helicopter Battalion, 40th Aviation
Brigade, 40th Infantry Division (Mechanized).
Stockton Army Aviation Support Facility,
Stockton Metropolitan Airport.**

Quickly removed but nevertheless protecting the
helicopter from the direction from which the
enemy is expected to come and preventing
unwanted glints from the cockpit canopy, the
use of partial camouflage with a net hanging
from the rotor is favoured when hasty take-offs
might be required

Left If this is war, count me in! An M60 gunner keeps a sharp look-out for fellow Guardsmen playing the role of enemy infiltrators seeking to overrun the forward site from which the 40th Attack Helicopter Battalion operated during a weekend drill in April 1987. **Above** Although the net still has to be hung around the tail boom and a rotor blade, this UH-1H has already almost blended into the background, thus demonstrating the effectiveness of this form of camouflage

Left This UH-1M (66-0494) of the 40th Atk Bn is seen fitted with launch rails for six AGM-22A anti-tank missiles, the French AS.11 wire-guided missiles which were built under licence in the United States during the late fifties and early sixties

Above As this refuelling scene was taken on 4 April 1987, before the start of the dry season, the background is still beautifully green

Overhauled by AVCRAD in Fresno and beautifully maintained by personnel of the 40th Attack Helicopter Battalion, this UH-1M built in 1966 appears to belie its age. Its AGM-22A missiles would, however, be obsolescent if not downright obsolete if used against the newer Soviet tanks. Being wire-guided, these missiles can be targeted against the softer armour aft of a tank's turret, but to do so the UH-1M has to remain out of natural cover for the gunner to keep the target in sight. Unfortunately, this also keeps the helicopter well in sight of enemy gunners

Skimming the ground, this Kiowa illustrates one of the helicopter's main shortcomings during field operations. Whether equipped with skids, like the UH-1 or the OH-58, or with low pressure tyres, like the CH-47 or the UH-60, helicopters cannot be taxied or towed across uneven ground. Hence, after operations were suspended and tactical considerations required that helicopters be moved from the main landing zone to dispersals among the trees, there was no other way to move this OH-58 but to have a pilot start its engine and fly it 300 metres across the Keystone Range meadows

Left Bucolic bliss: Accustomed to the flop-flop noise of rotors, 'beeffalo' (a cross between a cow and a buffalo) cattle keep on grazing as an OH-58A flies low over the Keystone Range meadow in the foothills of the Sierras

1st Squadron of the 18th Cavalry, 40th Aviation Brigade, 40th Infantry Division (Mechanized). Los Alamitos Army Aviation Support Facility, Los Alamitos Airfield.

Above As the Camp Roberts' gunnery range is used frequently, it has well prepared sites such as this one featuring concrete helipads on the bluff overlooking the firing range. Nevertheless, dust can be a serious factor during summer day operations. Fortunately, range safety observers can still do their job effectively as they stand in an observation tower located sufficiently aft from the landing zone to remain clear of the dust

Overleaf Flames belch out from the GAU-2B Minigun as this UH-1M of Troop D, 1/18 Cavalry, 'stitches the ground' with 7.62 mm bullets during gun firing practice at Camp Roberts

35

An UH-1M fitted with the XM21 weapons system (seven-round rocket launcher and Minigun on each side of the fuselage) returns to the pad after its crew has completed refresher training by firing the prescribed number of 2.75 mm rockets. For Guard crews, this is an easy task as most of them are Vietnam veterans with ample experience firing rockets during operations against the VC and NVA

The 1/18 Cavalry and the 40th Attack Helicopter Battalion will both have to continue training with obsolete UH-1Ms until active Army units have a sufficient number of AH-64A Apache helicopters to release AH-1S Cobras for Guard and Reserve units. Meanwhile, no funds have been found to equip the Guard's UH-1Ms with IR suppression jetpipe, chaff/flare dispensers or IRCM jammers, thus leaving them as easy prey in the event of war

At the end of a day on the gunnery range, 65-9504 sweeps away from another UH-1M of the 1/18 Cavalry

The forward fuselage of this UH-1M is fitted with an M5 ball turret housing an M75 40 mm grenade launcher. The rounds are carried in a cannister inside the cabin, with feed chutes leading forward between the pilots' seats. This Huey gunship also carries M158 launchers for seven 2.75-in rockets

Bearing the serial 72-21364, this OH-58A Kiowa has the upper portion of its vertical fin adorned with the traditional crossed sabres of the US Cavalry

An OH-58A hovering while its pilot makes a final
check prior to the start of a scouting mission

Above Three of the 12 OH-58As of the 1/18 Cavalry are lined-up on the airfield at East Garrison, Camp Roberts. The forward-slanting, yellow-tipped devices above and below the cabin are cable cutters

California Aviation Classification and Repair Activity Depot (AVCRAD). Fresno Air Terminal

Left AVCRAD provides maintenance depot activities not only for the 145 helicopters (90 UH-1H/M/Vs, 37 OH-58As, 16 CH-47A/B/Cs, and two EH-1Xs) and five fixed-wing aircraft (two C-7As, one C-12D, and two T-42As) of the CA ArNG but also for those from all Army Guard units in 12 western states and some from active duty units. Other AVCRAD facilities are located in Biloxi, Mississippi; Groton, Connecticut; and Springfield, Missouri

Preceding page The recently completed AVCRAD facility in Fresno has a floor area of 85,000 sq ft (8000 m²) and a permanent staff of 100 people. In addition, 20 specialists are employed temporarily as the California AVCRAD is currently overhauling and rebuilding AH-1S Cobra attack helicopters which are to be assigned to Guard units in the western states

Following the acquisition of a trial batch of seven Caribou STOL transports, the US Army acquired 159 production aircraft, which were initially designated AC-1s and AC-1As and which became CV-2As and CV-2Bs in 1962 prior to being deployed to Vietnam. All surviving Caribou transports were transferred to the USAF in 1967 and shortly thereafter were redesignated C-7As and C-7Bs. All have now been phased out by the Air Force but a few have been returned to Army service, including two operated by the California AVCRAD to fly parts to Guard units in 13 western states

When the sprawl of urban housing rendered jet operations from the Naval Air Station Los Alamitos untenable due to environmental considerations, the Navy vacated this facility and the California Army National Guard moved in with its less noisy helicopters. The Guard units operating from Los Alamitos are the 1st Squadron of the 18th Cavalry, the 140th Combat Support Aviation Company, the 340th General Support Aviation Company, and the 1240th Transportation Aviation Maintenance Company with a total of 67 UH-1s and OH-58s

Top left California ArNG helicopter pilots receive initial and refresher night flying training with AN/PVS-5 night vision goggles (NVGs) at Camp Roberts where a specialized detachment is located. An UH-1H from this 'Midnight Operations' unit is shown here on the ramp after being serviced in preparation for that night's training flight

Left Two UH-1X helicopters, equipped for detecting and jamming enemy radio communications, are assigned to the California Army National Guard and operated from the Fresno Army Aviation facility. The little-known UH-1Xs, modified from UH-1H airframes, are flown as three-seaters with most of the aft cabin filled with electronic gear and the operator's

station. Twin *Quick Fix* dipole aerials are on each side of the tail boom. This EH-1X (69-15936) is also fitted with IR suppression exhaust and a chaff/flare dispenser on each side of the fuselage

Above For liaison and light transport duties, the California Army National Guard has three Beech twin-engined aircraft, a turboprop-powered C-12D and two piston-powered T-42As. This Cochise (65-12730) was photographed on 5 May 1987 from the control tower at the Los Alamitos Army Airfield

194th Fighter Interceptor Squadron, 144th Fighter Interceptor Wing. Fresno Air Terminal.

Left A pair of F-4Ds returning to the 144th FIW base in Fresno is caught banking over the rich agricultural land of the San Joaquin Valley

Above After flying F-106A/Bs for almost ten years, the 194th FIS completed its conversion to F-4Ds in early 1984. This F-4D-28-MC was photographed one year later over a cloud bank off the coast of California, west of Carmel

Overleaf In 1986–87, aircraft and crews from the 194th FIS joined those from other Guard units at Ramstein AB in Germany to form the ANG Detachment 11 which took over alert duty from the 86th TFW while this USAFE unit converted from F-4Es to F-16Cs. However, 66-0747 was photographed in the clearer skies of California before the Guardsmen picked up their TDY assignment in Europe

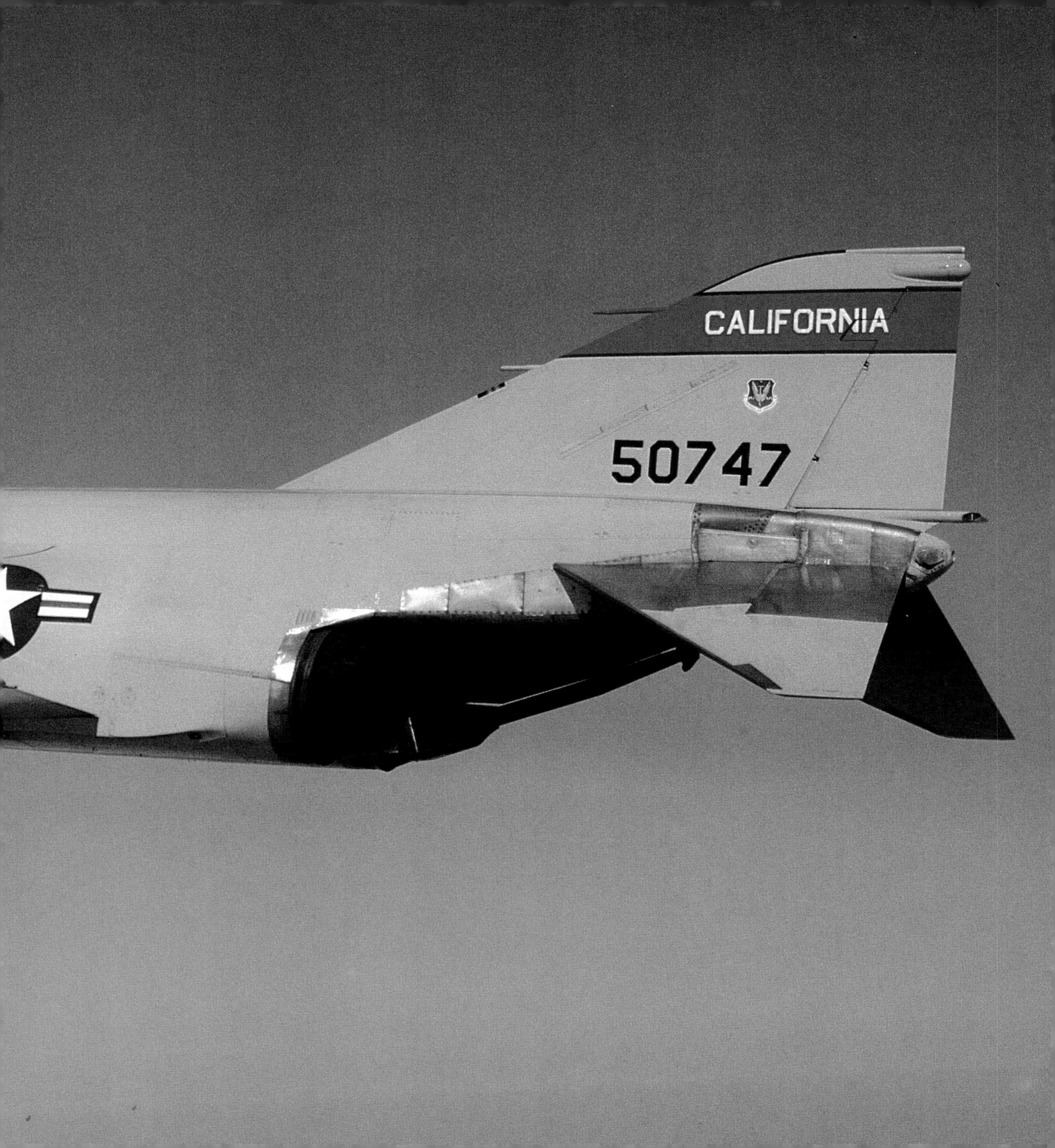
CALIFORNIA
50747

Above Noteworthy in this view of the rear fuselage and tail surfaces of 65-0747 is the hefty arrester hook, a sure sign of the F-4Ds naval ancestry. The griffin insignia on the right side of the fin is that of the 194th FIS; that of the Tactical Air Command appears in the same location on the left side

Right Armed with a single AIM-9P Sidewinder air-to-air missile during a sortie on 23 February 1985, 66-0269 was still finished in the Vietnam-era camouflage in which the 194th FIS received most of its F-4Ds

Top left In the spring of 1987, the 194th FIS was equipped with F-4Ds finished in three different camouflage schemes, two of which are seen in this view taken from the roof of the maintenance hangar. As shown in the next photograph, other aircraft were then finished in the so-called 'European One' scheme

Left Caught in the rays of the late afternoon sun on a clear spring day, 65-0667 shows off the various shades of grey and green of its 'European One' camouflage as it taxies out of the Guard ramp at the Fresno Air Terminal

Above Before aircraft are removed from alert status to undergo routine servicing, all armament, such as this AIM-7D Sparrow missile, has to be unloaded

Above Whereas during the 1950's and 1960's the Air Defense Command had several hundred interceptors in service with active squadrons and was supplemented by ANG squadrons, today the nation no longer feels a need for a large force of interceptors. Thus, air defence of heavily populated Southern California is provided by only two F-4Ds from Det 1 of the 144th FIW operating from TAC facilities at George AFB. One of these F-4Ds is seen returning to the alert shelter at the end of a mock interception on 12 August 1986

Right After receiving its first Lockheed T-33A jet trainers in September 1954, the 194th FIS was forced to move from the noise-sensitive Hayward Municipal Airport to its present base in Fresno. Ever since, the unit has operated a few T-33As along with its interceptors but the days of the Lockheed trainers are now numbered; all T-33As in USAF service are to be phased out before the end of March 1988. One of the last T-33As of the 194th FIS, 56-1586, was photographed off the coast of California on 23 February 1985 while flown by Col Allen W Boone

196th Tactical Fighter Squadron, 163rd Tactical Fighter Group. March AFB.

Photographed in January 1984 and already looking sharp after having been the recipient of much Guard TLC (tender loving care), this F-4C (63-7510) was one of the rather tired Phantom IIs which the 163rd TFS inherited from the 58th Tactical Training Wing at Luke AFB during the previous year

The star-studded markings carried by Phantom IIs of the 163rd TFS are a carry-over from the days when this distinctive heraldry was first applied to Delta Darts of the unit's forebear, the 163rd Fighter Interceptor Squadron

Top Receiving brand new Lockheed F-80Cs in June 1948, the 163rd Fighter Squadron became the first Guard unit anywhere in the nation to undergo jet conversion. However, this proud heritage was nearly lost during the mid-seventies anti-war era when many forgot that jet noise is the sound of freedom and the squadron was forced to exchange its 787-mph F-102As for 199-mph O-2As. After eight years in purgatory and a move to the less noise sensitive March AFB, the 163rd converted back to jets and, equipped with F-4Cs, became a Tactical Fighter Squadron in 1983

Left Carrying a pair of 370-gallon (1400-litre) drop tanks, 63-7426 is seen departing the ramp at the start of a navigation training sortie in January 1984

63

Above As three F-4Cs hold before taxying to the active runway at March AFB on 7 August 1986, ground personnel check the aircraft and remove safety pins. The pilot and WSO of the aircraft in the foreground keep their hands on the canopy frame, away from switches and toggles, to show the ground crew that it is safe to go underneath the aircraft and in front of weapons

Below Old warriors never die, they only test away. Still bearing the tail markings of its former operator, the 163rd TFG with which it served until the middle of 1987 when the March AFB unit completed its conversion to F-4Es, this F-4C-19-MC (N42IFS, ex-63-7545) is now operated by Flight Systems Inc. It was photographed at Mojave Airport on 19 August 1987

Overleaf An F-4C, 64-0783, flown by Majors Ron Cardin and Bruce Gillis, and two F-4Es, 68-0409 and 68-0367, respectively flown by 2Lt Scott Combest and Captain Bruce Johnson and by 1Lt Jon Proehl and Captain Rich Perez, fly over the cloud covered San Bernardino Mountains. The photo plane, an F-4C, was flown by Lt Col Dick Nester, the commander of the 163rd TFS

Above Transition time: after flying F-4Cs for four years, the 163rd TFS converted to F-4Es during the spring of 1987. Less than a month after this photograph was taken on 20 May, the last of the F-4Cs had been retired, most going to museums

Left Carrying a 600-gallon (2271-litre) ventral tank and MER racks with practice bombs, 68-0409 breaks away from 64-0783

Top left Returning from a dive bombing training sortie, 68-0367, a 19-year-old F-4E, shows off its new grey-on-grey scheme. By then, the 50-year old photographer was looking considerably paler, nay greener

115th Tactical Airlift Squadron, 146th Tactical Airlift Wing. Van Nuys ANGB.

Photographed on 17 June 1987 during a fire-fighting training sortie in the Rouse Ridge area of the San Bernardino National Forest, this Hercules is seen dumping a load of water at the start of its push-over manoeuvre as it dives toward the 'fire.' Had this been a real fire, the water would have been mixed with Monsanto 'Phos-Check' retardant and the plume would have been red instead of white. Push-overs are normally initiated 150 to 200 ft (45 to 60 m) above a ridge at a speed of 110 to 140 knots (205 to 260 km/h)

Above Developed by FMC Corporation, the MAFFS (Modular Airborne Fire Fighting System) can be installed in a C-130 in less than two hours and enables Hercules to drop 3000 US gallons (11,355 litres) of fire retardant in six to eight seconds over an area 150 ft (45 m) wide and 2000 ft (610 m) long. The fire retardant/water mixed is discharged through the two nozzles protruding from the aft ramp

Left Air Force Reservists from the 943rd TAG and Guardsmen from California's 115th TAS, North Carolina's 156th TAS, and Wyoming's 187th TAS got together at March AFB in June 1987 for a week of practice aerial fire fighting in anticipation of the fire season. The eight participating aircraft, plus a replacement aircraft sent later by the 115th TAS, received temporary day-glow numbers: 4 and 8 were sent by the CA ANG, I came from Wyoming, and 2 belonged to the locally-based AFRES unit

Above During the fire season, generally between mid-May and mid-October, the 115th TAS keeps two C-130Es and MAFFS-trained crews ready to answer requests from the US Forest Service

Right Under the watchful eyes of the crew chief, engines are about to be started before the day's first sortie. The wing's emblem, over which the last four digits of the aircraft's serial number have been painted, can be seen in one of the lower cockpit windows on the right side

As it drones on final approach to March AFB, 62-1851 shows off its temporary numerals and markings on the leading edges of the wings and tailplanes. The external tanks and pylons normally carried beneath the wings have been removed to reduce weight and increase manoeuvrability during the demanding fire fighting mission, thus leaving a light coloured area between each pair of engines

After one of the two C-130Es it had sent to take
part in the MAFFS training exercise came down
with maintenance problems, the 115th TAS
quickly replaced it with 61-2367

In honour of its crew chief, P Gonzales, this C-130E (61-2367) bears a rendering of the well-known 'Speedy Gonzales' cartoon forward of its crew entrance door. The XX on the bottle held by 'Speedy' reflects a certain liking for the Mexican beer 'Dos Equis', a favourite beverage on a hot California summer day

Flying a regular transport mission in October
1985, this C-130E comes in for a landing at
McClellan AFB, the sprawling Air Force
Logistics Command base on the outskirts of
Sacramento

Bearing the serial 62-1842, this C-130E of the 115th TAS taxies in front and below the control tower at McClellan AFB on 26 February 1984. *(Carl E Porter)*

129th Aerospace Rescue and Recovery Squadron, 129th Aerospace Rescue and Recovery Group. NAS Moffet Field.

The 129th ARRG regularly deploys its Hercules to Europe and the Far East to provide quarterly AR (air refuelling) training for rescue helicopter squadrons operating in support of USAFE and PACAF. This HC-130P (66-0221) was photographed at Andersen AFB, Guam, on 22 October 1982, as it was on its way to Osan AB, Korea, to work with the HH-3Es of the 38th ARRS

Overleaf Unlike the HC-130P, the HC-130H version is not equipped to refuel helicopters. Hence, it does not carry the HRUs (Hose Refuelling Units) mounted outboard of the engines and housing 83 ft of hose and a refuelling basket. *(Carl E Porter)*

Assigned the call sign KING 83 and photographed at NAS Moffett Field on 15 May 1982, 65-0983 is one of the two HC-130Hs currently operated by the 129th ARRG. Since it was given the rescue mission in 1975, the 129th has been credited with saving 167 lives, including 44 in 1986 and 18 during the first half of 1987. *(Peter B Lewis)*

In 1975, when the 129th became a rescue unit
equipped with Hercules, such as 66-0221 taxying
at McClellan AFB in January 1976, and Jolly
Green Giants, its aircraft and helicopters were
finished in the then traditional Aerospace
Rescue and Recovery Service scheme: light
grey overall with a black-bordered yellow
fuselage band. *(Carl E Porter)*

Above Flying at 150 kts (275 km/h) and 2500 ft (760 m), JOLLY 07 takes on 500 lb (290 litres) of JP4 from KING 04 during a training sortie off the California coast south of San Francisco on the afternoon of 10 September 1987. If Congress approves the Air Guard request for new equipment, JOLLY 07, an HH-3E bearing the serial 66-13284, and the four other helicopters (three HH-3Es and a CH-3E) currently assigned to the 129th ARRS will be replaced within two years by brand new Sikorsky MH-60s

Right As part of its on-going operations, the 129th ARRS provides water rescue training for U-2, TR-1, and SR-71 aircrews of the 9th Strategic Reconnaissance Wing. Wearing an S-1010B pressure suit, this TR-1 pilot and his 'rescuer' ride the penetrator hoist while being winched aboard a Jolly Green during a training exercise at Lake Engebretsen in the foothills of the Sierra Nevada, near the 9th SRW home at Beale AFB

On display at Beale AFB in May 1978, this HH-3E shows the external tanks and refuelling probe which characterize this version of the Sikorsky S.61. In the refuelling position, this probe extends forward 4 ft (1.22 m) to keep the tanker's basket and hose out of the way of the rotor. *(Carl E Porter)*

Left Still serving with the 129th ARRG six years after this photograph was taken in June 1981, 65-12781 has now been repainted in the European One camouflage scheme. *(Carl E Porter)*

Above Photographed in front of one of the old dirigible hangars at NAS Moffett Field, 66-0224 is about to depart on another rescue mission on 24 April 1987

Warriors and Saviours

Left MSgt Cline C Jack, Aircrew Life Support Superintendent, proudly wears the Zulu Warrior chest patch of the Guard men and women who have been part of the ANG Detachment 11 at Ramstein AB, Germany

Above The technical prowess of ground personnel from the Guard cannot be questioned: regardless of age, aircraft, engines, and systems always have a 'factory fesh' look after having been refurbished and maintained by these dedicated men and women. Although it is nearly 20-years old and has seen much use, this J79-GE-15 is as clean as a whistle

Experience is one of the main strengths of the Guard and enables it to excel when participating in Air Force competitions. There is no doubt that TSgt Robert S McGarigle, a veteran from the 144th FIW, has far more savvy than weapons control systems mechanics freshly graduated from the Chanute Technical Training Center and assigned to an active unit for their first tour of duty

When the 194th FIS converted from single-seat
F-106As to two-seat F-4Ds at the beginning of
1984, it suddenly needed to find or train some
30 WSOs (weapon systems officers). Major Jim
Thompson is one of the 'back-seaters' who then
came to Fresno from Guard units in other
states, in this case the 178th FIS of the North
Dakota Air National Guard

Lt Col Roy S Stuckey, the Squadron Operations Officer, is still strapped on the Martin-Baker Mk-H7 seat in the front cockpit of an F-4D of the 194th FIS as he goes through the check list before engine shut down at the end of a sortie on 9 April 1987

On 23 April 1987, five PJs (pararescue jumpers) of the 129th ARRS jumped from an HC-130P some 2000 miles from the California coast to come to the rescue of three severely burned crew members of an ocean tug. Two of the PJs, TSgt Randall W Wilkinson and SSgt Mark A Schneider, were photographed two days later at NAS Alameda after their superb efforts had stabilized the condition of the three victims. Unfortunately, one of the three sailors died after his transfer to a specialized burn centre

Above Remarkably resilient after the 48-hour ordeal aboard the *Marine Constructor*, TSgt Timothy J Williams details the procedures that he and the four other PJs used to save the burn victims. After jumping into the ocean and boarding the ocean tug, the PJs received advice over the radio from Captain John G Soto, a flight surgeon from the 129th ARRS, and from Dr William DeCampli, a civilian burn specialist from the Stanford University Medical Center, who were aboard the HC-130P circling overhead

Right SSgt Rodrigo Dezubria, another of the courageous and skilled PJs who participated in the rescue mission on 23/25 April, exudes both fatigue and satisfaction after returning to NAS Alameda aboard the Grumman C-2A which flew the victims, four of the PJs, and Navy medics from the USS *Ranger* to the mainland. The fifth PJ, A1C Michael J Stasio, remained on board the *Ranger* for two more days. He came back aboard the HH-3E of the 129th ARRS which had returned to the USS *Ranger* on the 24th to provide transportation for the victims in the event the Navy could not supply the C-2A needed for a smoother and faster flight

Left Had the C-2A not been available, the HH-3E would have had to be refuelled several times to reach the coast. To provide AR in this eventuality, the 129th ARRS dispatched two HC-130Ps (one of which belonged to an active unit, the 1550th CCTW, and was flown by Air Force personnel from Kirtland AFB). Major John W Duncan, Jr, one of the navigators from the 129th, is seen working aboard 66-0224 during this mission

Above Standing near the left-hand troop door in the aft end of an HC-130P during a flight over the Pacific, MSgt Curtiss A Welle, loadmaster, and MSgt Allan Williams, a para-rescue jumper, review procedures in preparation for dropping two PJs near the location from which aircraft distress signals have been reported to emanate

99

Left After donning a Soviet tunic and helmet, an NCO of the 40th Attack Helicopter Battalion instructs his fellow Guardsmen on proper techniques for frisking prisoners. In this instance, however, the 'prisoner' does not appear to be overly concerned

Above Although flying helicopters is where their heart is, Army National Guard pilots—in Nomex flight suit and 'brain bucket'—must, just like common 'ground pounders' in camouflaged fatigue, hone their skill with personal firearms. Obviously, not everyone enjoys that chore . . .

In addition to her normal duty with the 126th Medical Company (Air Ambulance), this flight medic assists the other crew members of an UH-1V by calling items from the check list as the Huey is being prepared for the morning's first flight at the Van Vleck Ranch in the foothills of the Sierras

Right Perhaps as many as 85 to 90 per cent of helicopter pilots serving with Army National Guard units are Vietnam veterans with an average of 2500 hours in their log book, including nearly 1000 hours of combat flying. Typical of these highly experienced Army Guard pilots is CW3 Philip R Westerlund, here keeping a sharp watch for traffic while his copilot does the flying on the way back to the 126th Medical Company's home facility at Mather AFB

Left Taking part in a chemical warfare exercise, this pilot of the 126th Medical Company wears the full NBC (Nuclear-Biological-Chemical) combat regalia, including standard issue infantry helmet, mask, and rubber gloves and booties. Hopefully to prove effective in the event of war, this protective gear is definitely cumbersome. Consequenlty, safety considerations mandate that in peacetime all NBC training flights be done with one pilot in full protective gear and the other in standard flight kit

Below Although it is a California National Guard facility, the AVCRAD depot in Fresno also handles overhauls and major repairs for aircraft and helicopters belonging to units in 12 other western states. Here, work is being done on the tail-rotor pylon of an UH-1D (66-1182) of the Montana National Guard

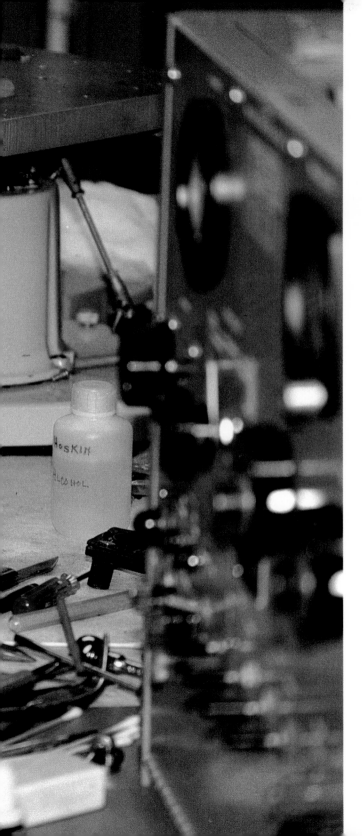

Above Conducted on 16–17 May 1987 in the foothills of the Sierras, this NBC exercise duplicated combat operations likely to prevail in Korea. Here a fully-equipped NCO struggles to plot troop movements on a map standing in the temporary operations centre erected under a tent. Fortunately for the participants, when this exercise took place, daytime temperatures had dropped to 85°F (29°C) from the high of 104°F (40°C) which had prevailed two days earlier

Skill, concentration and, again, experience are well in evidence as this AVCRAD specialist fine tunes flight instruments prior to their re-installation in an UH-1

Left Standing next to the 2200 shp T55-L-5 turboshaft on the right side of a CH-47A being preflighted prior to a ferry flight from Camp Irwin to Camp San Luis Obispo on a windy winter day, WO1 William D Craig catches a bite on the run. A proper meal came much later for Bill and his Guard fellows from the *Delta Schooners* as they ran into a bit of nasty weather near Santa Margarita. Experience and knowing when to turn back paid handsomely as the flight ended with a splendid and good spirited dinner

Even an unusually cold and windy winter day at Bicycle Lake cannot put a dent in the good humour of Sgt Joe L Perez as he lubricates the aft rotor drive shaft of 63-7911, a Chinook of the 49th Combat Aviation Company

The Good Old Days

Left At one time or another between 1946 and 1957, no fewer than 75 out of the 98 Guard squadrons—including four in California, the 115th, 194th, 195th, and 197th—flew Mustangs. Flown by Brig Gen John Felton Turner, the commander of the 144th Fighter Wing, this F-51D is seen flying over a typical early summer San Francisco fog bank on 24 June 1951. *(William T Larkins)*

Above This North American F-86L (52-4112) displays on its fin the griffin squadron insignia of the Fresno-based 194th FIS as it is towed away during the 1963 Armed Forces Day air show at Hamilton AFB. *(Peter B Lewis)*

No aviation pictorial book is complete without at least one photograph of a Douglas C-47! Then serving as the state's VIP and staff transport, this VC-47A-85-DL (43-15579) was photographed at McClellan AFB, a short automobile ride from the State Military Department headquarters in Sacramento, on 17 September 1967. *(Peter B Lewis)*

During the fifties and sixties, the California Army National Guard operated a number of de Havilland Beaver communications and light transport aircraft, including this U-6A photographed in Fresno on 7 April 1968. *(Peter B Lewis)*

Grumman Albatross amphibians were assigned to the 129th Troop Carrier Squadron (Medium) between late 1956 and the summer of 1963. Still bearing its CALIF AIR GUARD markings on the hull, this HU-16A (49-0088) was photographed in the 'boneyard' at Davis-Monthan AFB on 13 March 1967, nearly four years after the type had been phased out by the 129th. *(Peter B Lewis)*

Overleaf Convair F-102A-30-CO (54-1382) of the 194th FIS during a stop-over at McClellan AFB on 17 September 1967. *(Peter B Lewis)*

Photographed at McClellan AFB on 24 May 1968, this U-10D was one of the Helio Super Courier STOL light transport aircraft which the 129th flew alongside Fairchild C-119s during most of the sixties and the first half of the seventies. *(Peter B Lewis)*

Finished in the aluminized acrylic lacquer which the USAF used briefly during the mid-sixties and early seventies, 57-0775, an F-102A-90-CO of the 196th FIS, is seen at its home base on 20 March 1970 with Mount Baldy in the background. *(Peter B Lewis)*

Overleaf This Convair TF-102A-30-CO of the 196th FIS at Ontario on 20 March 1970 shows off the characteristic air intakes of the two-seat training version of the Delta Dagger. Interestingly, this intake configuration has been revived by Dassault for its most recent fighter, the Rafale. *(Peter B Lewis)*

Preceding pages This Lockheed C-130A (55-0013) of the 115th TAS was photographed at Van Nuys in April 1971. Nineteen months later, it was one of 32 Hercules hastily handed over to the VNAF as part of *Enhance Plus*, the transfer of military equipment undertaken to strengthen South Vietnamese forces before the US military withdrawal from Vietnam. It was captured by the NVA in April 1975 and is assumed to have later been operated by the Vietnam People's Air Force

Below Although the militarized version of the Cessna 337 Skymaster performed well in the FAC role during the Vietnam War, the conversion from F-102As to O-2As was hard to take for the fighter jocks of the 196th. Photographed at Ontario on 11 May 1975, 67-21465 is noteworthy as it was the last of the 31 commercial aircraft purchased by the Air Force for use in the psychological warfare role. The leaflet dispenser initially fitted on the rear starboard side of these O-2Bs had by then been removed and the standard entrance door on that side replaced with a door featuring an additional window. *(Peter B Lewis)*

By the time the last T-33As are phased out in
March 1988, the type will have been operated
continuously by California Air National Guard
squadrons for almost 34 years. This is indeed
quite a tribute to the design soundness of
Lockheed's first jet aircraft. The XP-80, from
which the two-seat T-33 trainer—then
designated TP-80C—was derived in 1947, had
first been flown in January 1944. This T-33A of
the 196th FIS was photographed at Ontario
Airport on 3 February 1973. *(Peter B Lewis)*

Overleaf As the last photographs for this book were being selected, the VIP/staff transport Convair C-131B (53-7791) of the California ANG was about to be replaced by a Beech C-12J. This long serving C-131B will then be donated to the museum at McClellan AFB, the base on the approach of which it was photographed on 27 May 1976. *(Peter B Lewis)*

Left For the men and women of the 144th FIW, as well as for aviation enthusiasts, the tail markings emulating the flag of the State of California and consisting of a golden bear on a white background with CALIFORNIA in black letters in a red band were among the most tasteful markings ever applied to military aircraft. This F-106B operational trainer (57-2535) is seen parked on the ramp at Fresno on 2 May 1982. *(Peter B Lewis)*

Above Profile of a superb interceptor: 58-0782 was photographed at Fresno in December 1975. The Delta Dart was the fourth type of jet fighter to be assigned to the 194th FIS since it began flying F-86As in October 1954. The unit converted to F-86Ls in 1958, to F-102As in 1964, and to F-106As in 1974. The last of their beloved F-106As (58-0774) departed Fresno for MASDC (Military Aircraft Storage & Disposition Center) at Davis-Monthan AFB on 18 January 1984. *(Peter B Lewis)*